A Season to Heal, A Season to Grow

Rick Moore

BookLeaf Publishing

India | USA | UK

Presentation by *BookLeaf Publishing*

Web: www.bookleafpub.com

E-mail: info@bookleafpub.com

ISBN: 9789358318050

First edition 2024

For Suzanne, if it weren't for you I would have given up a long time ago.

ACKNOWLEDGEMENT

My wife Suzanne has taken care of me in innumerable ways, especially since my injury. I can never repay all that she has done. But that doesn't mean I won't try.

My mom and dad gave me a childhood full of books and read to me until I could do it for myself. They planted the seeds of this book many years ago.

PREFACE

When I woke up in the hospital a few years ago with my legs paralyzed, my first feelings weren't despair or sadness, though those feelings came and still come around. I was thankful to still be in this world alive, and hopeful that I could overcome any challenges set before me. I had no idea how much work would be involved. I'm still on that journey that I started that day, and I don't know if my life will ever be anything like it was before. But I have found pieces of my old life and stitched them together with this new life and created something that is beginning to feel like me again.

These poems are a part of that healing process. I have written poetry since I was a young boy and though I dreamed of someday publishing some collection of my work, I always thought of it as a silly and frivolous thing. I put my energy into songwriting instead, as a more practical and popular way to share my lyrical thoughts. But here I put aside the need for chorus and verse and rhyme patterns and focus on my sincere thoughts and feelings to share how I have come to see the world and my place in this universe as an adult reborn into life. The idea of rebirth through baptism is fundamental to Christianity, but it is also written into the laws of nature. It's not an easy process and it's a work in progress, but I will keep building my new life.

In the Beginning...

How lonely was that first cell?
Such a longing for connection
That led to you and me
And all the trees
The dinosaurs
Bumblebees and snails
Every heart that ever beat
And every leaf that ever fell.

Scar Tissue

Wounds so deep the body must memorialize
As if the skin was welded together
Then left raw and ragged
That pink ribbon
So soft and sensitive
A delicate reminder of pain
A knee cut on the swing set at age 7
The leg that was bitten by the neighbor's dog in
4th grade
A few places where the barbed wire scratched
me cutting through the fences in the pasture
Knuckles that bear the marks of high school
shop class sander
And now this zipper up my back where my spine
was laid open and put back together again
A scar is proof of the body's drive to remain
whole
To fill in the broken places the best it can
Never quite the same

Forgiveness

There's nothing instinctive about forgiveness
It requires a careful rewiring of the circuitry of
your mind
To look at someone who has harmed you
And see past the pain they caused
And to believe that things can get better
And to hope that the wound won't be repeated
Yet in a world of endless possibilities
And one in which change is the most constant
principle
In a universe in a perpetual state of flux
How God-like it is
To open your heart and make room
For the best version of those who you love to
show up and shine

Hurry Scurry

Hurry, scurry squirrel and see
Acorns dropped from this great tree
Winter soon will come and freeze
But warm and safe I'm sure you'll be

Run and gather now my friend,
Autumn's days will quickly end
And harvest time won't come again
Til we've gone round our orbit's bend.

Hurry, scurry squirrel and see
The sun shines bright on you and me
And each of us is just as free
And just as greatly blessed.

So Much

She must be the sun
Because her smile makes me want to grow and
be more
Or perhaps the moon
For the way she tugs the tides of my heart.
She could be the stars spilling across the sky into
infinity
To light my way home no matter how far I
wander.
Or the Earth
My home, my refuge, my foundation.
She's all that and more,
Because she is my universe
Within me and without me from here to the end
of time and space
My everything that was and will be.

Purr and Fur

She said, "we're getting a kitten."
And I learned long ago that this was not an
opening to a discussion but simply a statement
of fact.
I defer to her in all matters feline
As an essential component of marital happiness.
I could have countered with logical objections.
Perhaps a complete refusal could have been
presented.
I may be stupid but I'm not a fool.

So we went to meet the kitten.
We had done so little together for too long
So seeing her smiling was the best thing ever
To be by her side as she found some joy
Was like the sun melting away the ice after a
storm
I could hear the dripping icicles in my soul
The kitten had a sister. So now we are getting
two.
She watched them play for maybe an hour.
Then we went back home to anticipate the
homecoming day.

Such a miniscule ball of fur and purr and love
soon found a home curled up under my chin
And in my lap
One chose me and the other chose her
Two sisters so different in looks and
temperament
But equal in cuteness. There's no better word.

And she was absolutely right again.
That kitten energy,
That extra five pounds of love and playfulness
Spread through our hearts and our home
Reminding us to find joy in the day
To make room for sweetness and cuddles
And everything is not perfect
But I think it's still getting better every day

Kintsugi

Broken and carefully mended
I will never be exactly the same as before
And I have tried to hide the ragged places
Like a wild thing afraid to let his weaknesses be
seen
Creeping off alone somewhere to lick my
wounds

But I am trying to shake off my primitive
thoughts
Leaving the cave and emerging into the light
blinking

How much more beautiful is hope
When you know that things can go horribly
wrong with no warning?
How much more precious is faith
When you know that not every prayer is
answered in the way you want?
How much greater is joy
When you have lived in the house of pain and
sadness until it became your home?

Petrichor

The dry earth was broken
Cracks like the fingerprint of death
All green turned to crisp yellow brown
Skeletal landscapes in the hazy sun
Hovering on the edge of combustion

I was broken too
The bleakness inside me as real as
The empty creek bed

When the rain began to fall
Everything was so dry that it couldn't penetrate
the skin
And when the clouds went on their way
The green only peeked again from the blazed
lawns

Now the rain has fallen for days
Flowers celebrate
Emerald flags are raised from every corner
Dust is washed away
And my whole being is captured by the scent of
a world brought back to vivid life

The Fly that Buzzes

Sometimes I get to the end of a thought, and all I
can do is cry.
I let it out, push it away, and keep going...
Like some fly that buzzes around my head
Because I know it will come back.
Some of the things that break my heart will keep
breaking it over and over and over.
There aren't cures or solutions or time machines
that can make it all better.
Some of the things that I lost I will miss forever.
I can't find some way back or search until I see
them again or even find a real replacement.
My dad is now made of memories and legacies.
I will never move over the Earth in the same free
way.
Years that I could have spent living one way
have been totally redirected into a path I would
have never chosen.
And that is a buzzing fly always in the room,
that never dies.
Sometimes it settles and I don't hear it.
Sometimes I can ignore it banging it's head
against the door.

Sometimes I want to smash it against the wall
and see it's guts smeared on some newspaper
roll.
And sometimes it just lands on my arm and I see
it's jeweled wings and round eyes staring at me
and I can at least be thankful my heart is still
beating enough to break.

Golden Elm

Nothing makes me feel
The passage of time
Quite like the slow sliding fall
Of the golden elm leaves

Resolute

Make room in your heart
For good things to happen.
Let the sun shine through the clouds
And find the quiet moments in the storm.
Worry is a habit that is hard to break,
And we're not made to carry tomorrow's burden.
Any hill is harder to climb
When you are focused on the peak.
Each moment is a part of the journey.
Be present and prepared.
Be ready for the miracles that can happen
When you meet your challenge
With sharpened sword
And a focused mind.

The Clarity of Peace

When anger and frustration clouds my eyes
I see only one path,
A super power when only one path is possible.
It's the gift of the Viking berserkers who gave
me my red hair
But in the world of choices I need to be nimble,
So I must breathe and reset
Finding the eye of the hurricane
And sitting cross-legged, palms open to the
world.
When I return to the battle I will be ready for all
possibilities.

The Heart Breaks Again

Sadness came in and sat down to breakfast with
me again
And when I remembered how long it's been
since you left I decided it could stay
This rock we're riding runs through the wake of
all our past pains
I can feel the angle of the rising sun and
recognize where we are in the story
There's no sense in skipping chapters
Even if it happens off stage it changes
everything

Rain on Familiar Soil

I've been here before
As the rain came in and the lightning reached
across the sky
But it has been so long
And I have seen the sky light up in bigger skies
Still I know from the feel of the skin on the back
of my arm
Exactly when the first drops will fall here.

Chrysalis

Hanging by a tiny string
Changing every tiny thing
Spreading out the brand new wings
Shining in the morning

Ouroboros

I've heard that everything that rises must
converge
That someday all who reach for the sun will be
as one
I've heard that every living being on this great
round rock
Can trace back to one single cell at the dawn of
life.
That great explosion that brought forth the
universe
Echoes into the uncertain future
Could there be a great nothing on the other side
of it all?
Life burns through my every cell so strong
That I can't believe in a world where it doesn't
persist.

Unplanned Goodbyes

The last time I saw my Grandpa we watched tv
"Where the seats are softer" as he always said
To invite you from the dining room to the living
room.
He told me stories about how much he loved my
Granny
And how hard they worked together to make a
life
When I had to leave he walked out with me
And our last hug was in that driveway

My Grandaddy Bill and I had breakfast with my
Dad
In the city where I learned to weld
And be a small part of the tradition of
generations
Of builders of great wheeled fortresses.
He ordered tea and when it was ready
He removed the bag carefully with a spoon
Wrapping the string around it and pressing with
the tag
Captured the last drops of goodness efficiently
In the same way that I always do
Though I'm sure I didn't learn it from him
directly.

We hugged in the parking lot one last time
The same awkward hug we'd always had

My Dad and I said goodbye at the airport
The same one where we'd dropped him off and
picked him up
For all those business trips he'd gone on
The same one where he'd dropped me off
For adventures as a young man
We spent the days before together watching
westerns
Sitting in the garage watching the rain as he
smoked
Mending the places where we'd hurt each other
We hugged each other tight
Trying to squeeze as hard as we loved each other

So many departures in this life
They can't all be perfect and most are unplanned
Unpredictable
I'm so thankful for the times when good bye
Has been given its moment without the pressure
of knowing it's finality

The Constance of Change

We're all standing in a river
The currents around us ripping away at the rocks
The still places harboring shadowy green
moments of life
Dashing fish move around our legs sometimes
seeking a taste
I plunge my face into the icy stream
My hands reaching and pulling through the
liquid
Struggling to move against the flow
Until I tire and submit
And allow it to carry me

The Promise in the Ring

When we stood beneath that tree
On a hot summer's evening
With the cries of cicadas in the air
I pledged myself to you and you to me
With bands of precious metals
Slipped onto our fingers as we spoke from our
hearts
So much has changed since that day
We've become different people
We live in a new land
We have lost things and people and parts of
ourselves
But I love the ways you have changed
And as I keep changing I want to be better for us
Let the promise of the ring be
That we always find our way
Back to each other

Living With Pain

I could never have appreciated my luck
To have lived a life of adventures and freedom
In a body strong and agile
To have tasted so many pleasures
And scaled mountain heights
To have danced the night away with women in
strange lands
And raced through the fields on horseback
And the million other ways that life was kind to
me

This constant ache that my broken body harbors
Reminds me of every joy that came so easily
And so I savor the moments of sweetness
Sometimes it takes a pinch of salt to make the
sugar sing

If Hope is a Thing With Wings

If hope is a thing with wings
Let it be the phoenix
Let it rise again and again
From the embers of its own destruction
Forged of something undeniable
It's not the bluebird singing a delicate song
Hope is a creature of fire and freedom
Leaping into the inky darkness
Inspiration brought to life.